GW00400011

CHIP CARVING

25 PROJECTS WITH INSTRUCTIONS AND FULL-SIZE PATTERNS

by Harris W. Moore

Dover Publications, Inc., New York

Directions for Playing Peg Morrel (See Project 14)

First one player then the other places a peg in a hole, each striving to get a "mill" (three pegs in a row but not cornerwise) and also to prevent his opponent from getting a mill. A mill entitles its owner to remove one opponent's peg, but not from any mill he may have. After all pegs have been placed, they are moved, without jumping, along the lines, one hole at a move. When a player has only three pegs left, he can jump anywhere; when he has only two, he has lost the game.

Directions for Playing Fox and Geese (See Project 15)

The fifteen geese are placed on the board in the holes that are indicated in black on the diagram. The fox is placed in the hole at the center of the board. The geese may move one space in any direction except diagonally. The fox may move in any direction except diagonally, and may also "jump" (as in checkers) a goose if the hole behind the goose is empty. If conditions are right, he may jump more than one goose. The geese win if they are able to block the fox so that he cannot move.

The problems of solitaire are various: one, for example, being to start with all holes filled except the center one, then to jump (and take up) all pegs except the last one, which is to land in the center hole. One or several holes in other parts of the board may be left empty, and so other problems created.

Published in Canada by General Publishing Company, Ltd., 30 Lesmill Road, Don Mills, Toronto Ontario.
Published in the United Kingdom by Constable and Company, Ltd.

This Dover edition, first published in 1976, is a revised republication of the work originally published by The Manual Arts Press, Peoria, Illinois, in 1922.

International Standard Book Number: 0-486-23256-5
Library of Congress Catalog Card Number: 75-19755

Manufactured in the United States of America
Dover Publications, Inc.
180 Varick Street, New York, N.Y. 10014

CONTENTS

INTRODUCTION

Historical Background

Chip carving, characterized as it is by angular incisions in the surface decorated, occupies a very limited field in the realm of wood carving. But with its limitations frankly recognized, it may appropriately be employed to enrich an otherwise plain surface. Because of its angularity, care must be exercised in applying it to curved surfaces or to surfaces having curved outlines, lest it become as degenerate as so many of our designs in cut glass have. Decoration by means of incisions has been utilized by many primitive peoples. While handling his weapons and implements in times of leisure, the primitive man would naturally turn to scratches and incisions as a method of embellishment. To appreciate what chip-carving may be at its best, one should see some of the ceremonial adz handles and paddles produced by the primitive men of the South Pacific islands. The decoration of these articles is characterized by an all-over pattern of small units, for the most part deeply cut. Often these units are as small as 1/8″ or 3/16″. The chief element in their beauty is repetition, and to achieve such beauty one must exercise great patience. As these articles were decorated for ceremonial occasion and not for daily use, no adaptations for convenience were necessary; some of the adz handles, for example, were hollow square tubes even as large as six inches on a side. Sharp corners and deep incisions were freely used. When we remember that these primitive craftsmen used a bit of shell or a shark's tooth as a cutting tool, we can appreciate better their devotion to their art. And let us always remember that without that devotion no beautiful thing is ever created.

Good examples of primitive design units are clearly shown in Figure 1. It is the varied combination of these units that produces the charm of the early carvings. In the best of these carvings there was always unity in the whole

Figure 1. Full-size units of primitive designs

scheme of decoration. Whatever the motif chosen, it was used consistently.

Although the Pacific Islands give us such beautiful examples of chip carving, we are indebted to the northern countries of Europe, including England and Ireland, where this style of decoration prevailed more than in southern Europe, for its influence upon our own craft work. Some churches in North Germany built in the eighth century show such carving in stone. In a church in Vaage, Norway, built before 1200 A.D., some of the pilasters show the strap or dragon pattern and some the incised geometric pattern. In Sweden, during the seventeenth and eighteenth centuries especially, this so-called peasant style or notch carving was widely applied to household furniture and implements. A rude knife, sometimes made from an old sword or scythe, was often the only tool used in making such carvings. This influence was largely transmitted to our own country through the sloyd schools established by Gustaf Larsson.

Tools and General Directions

Although all the designs suggested in this book can be cut with the chip-carving knife shown in Figure 2, the following additional tools will be found convenient: a wood carver's veining tool, Figure 3; a parting tool 1/32" to 1/16" wide, Figure 4; and a 1" skew chisel, Figure 5, for the larger chips. In flower-form rosettes, as in Project 20, a carver's gouge of proper curve shown in Figure 6 is helpful for stabbing. These cutting tools should be honed to a keen, perfect edge on a fine sharpening stone, stropped on leather, and then protected from all injury by sticking them into corks when not in use. Results can be attained with perfect cutting tools which are simply unattainable with dull ones. For the single purpose of veining (cutting narrow grooves), the veining tool should be sharpened so that the cutting edges of the V slant forward somewhat so that they cut the wood just ahead of the point of the V as shown in Figure 3. Only in this shape will this tool cut smoothly across the grain.

Since the designs in this book are all full size, it is expected that they will be traced and transferred to the model by carbon paper. Should they not be traced, the following drawing tools will be needed: T-square, 45° triangle, 30° x 60° triangle, 22-1/2° x 67-1/2° triangle, compass, divider, scroll, and ruler. Angles of 15° and 75° can be obtained by adding the 30° angle to the 45° triangle.

After one has acquired considerable skill in carving, not all the lines shown in the design need be drawn, for some of them will result from stabbing and some from cutting the chips. In general the important point to lay out is the point where the knife is set to stab the design.

The first cutting operation is to stab the design, making a vertical cut, the point of the knife being at the deepest part of the incision to be made,

Figure 2. Knife

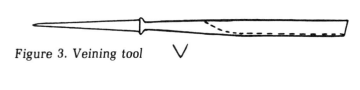

Figure 3. Veining tool   V

Figure 4. Parting tool   ∪

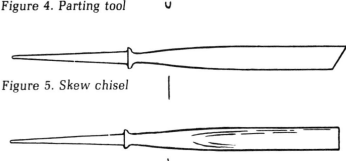

Figure 5. Skew chisel |

Figure 6. Carver's gouge   )

Figure 7. Stabbing

Figure 7. Care must be taken to hold the knife vertical and make the stab coincide with the lines of the pattern. To remove the chip, the knife is held as in Figure 8 with the thumb held firmly on the work to serve as a sort of pivot on which to swing the hand while forcing the blade of the knife under the chip. In doing this the point of the knife must be kept from going into the vertical wall made by the stab, or into an adjoining chip. Small chips in straight grain wood should be removed at one cut; large ones, curved ones, or those in crooked grain may require two

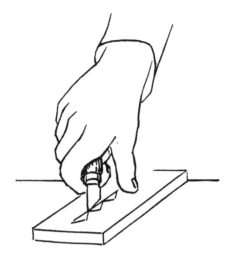

Figure 8. Removing chips

or more cuts to remove the chip smoothly. A smooth, crisp, clear-cut chip is the only one which should give satisfaction; but one should not give up if this is not obtained with the first trial, for sometimes unsuccessful cuts can be improved by recutting deeper.

In these plates dimensions are always given in the following order: length, width, thickness. The sign for inches is omitted because no model is large enough to require measurement by feet.

Two parallel lines close together (about 1/32) represent a groove. Grooves may be cut with knife, parting tool, or veiner. In the attempt to indicate the valleys, (the deep incisions), by shading, the light is supposed to come from the upper left corner of the page. Before stabbing any pattern, one must have clearly in mind what chips are to be cut out.

Sparklets (little V-shape cuts in the edge of a chip as shown in Project 16) are best cut with the knife held nearly vertical.

To add crispness to the carved pattern, it is sometimes necessary to stab it all again and thus clearly emphasize the deep places, the divisions between cuts.

In the selection of wood for the various articles illustrated in this book, the following considerations are pertinent. The soft, close-grain woods cut easier than the hard woods, but if subjected to hard usage they do not wear as well. For an article which is used rather intimately

and viewed close by, a choice wood is appropriate. Some of the soft woods are pine, basswood, poplar or whitewood, and red-gun; those of medium hardness, mahogany and black walnut; the hard woods, cherry, oak, birch and hard maple. Of course, some trees of any of these kinds vary one way or the other from the average of its kind. Although carved wood may be stained or dyed it is generally better to select wood of natural beauty, and to finish it without stain. Color, however, is such an important element of beauty and harmony that one should not hesitate to use the excellent commercial wood stains and dyes which are now available, if thereby the article is made more harmonious with its surroundings.

Before wood is finished it should be smooth and clean. No attempt should be made to sandpaper the actual cuts of a piece of chip carving. The tools should be sharp enough and used with such precision as to leave the surface smooth. If a surface needs sandpapering after it has been carved, the sandpapering should be done carefully with fine sandpaper wrapped snugly about a smooth flat block; and this should be moved in the direction of the grain. Great care is needed not to flatten the sharp ridges of the carving.

For articles which are not to be handled much, a wax or linseed oil finish is suitable. Dull rather than glossy finish should be used. An article that is apt to become soiled with handling and hence need cleaning at times is better finished with shellac or varnish. Thin white shellac laid on quickly with a soft camel's hair brush makes a good, hard finish. Shellac is not waterproof but turns white in a few hours under water.

A wax finish is easily obtained with the commercial prepared waxes or with beeswax cut with turpentine till a soft paste results. These waxes may be brushed on and then polished after a little time with a brush as shoes are polished. A good durable finish may be obtained in the course of several weeks by the use of linseed oil alone if successive applications of oil are rubbed well with a cloth and allowed to dry thoroughly between applications. Sometimes a week is not too long a time to allow the oil to harden.

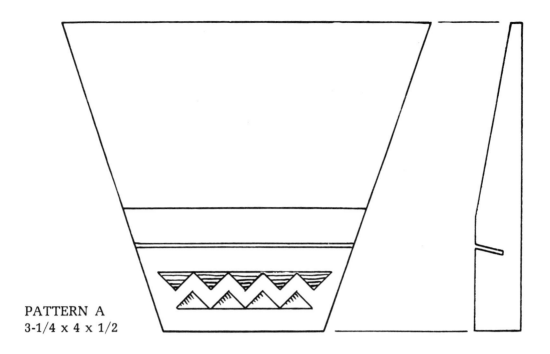

PATTERN A
3-1/4 x 4 x 1/2

PATTERN B   4-1/4 x 2-1/2 x 3/4

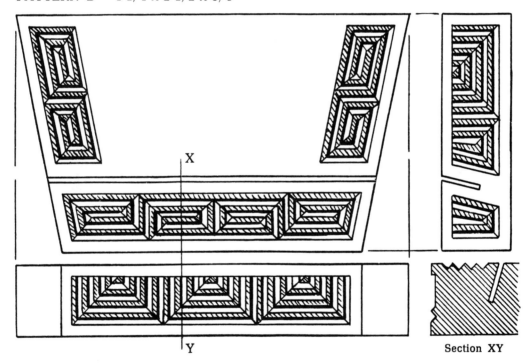

X

Y

Section XY

Projects 1 and 2
EASELS FOR HOLDING PHOTOGRAPHS OR POST CARDS

A. The grain of the wood in this easel should run vertically as shown in this plate. One should not attempt to carve any pattern until one has succeeded in carving the design on a practice piece of wood. The model may or may not be planed thin at the wide end.

B. The heavy line indicating the valley and the miter lines at the corners are the important lines in the lay-out of this design. The carving of this pattern should start at the inner end of the fret, care being taken not to cut across any ridge. The sectional drawing shows ridges and valleys.

Repeat patterns A, B, or C on each side.

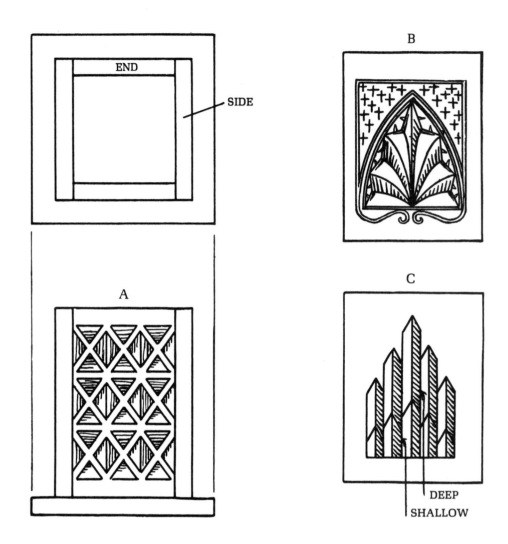

BOTTOM 2 x 2 x 3/16   SIDES 2 x 1-1/2 x 3/16   ENDS 2 x 1/8 x 3/16

Projects 3, 4 and 5
HOLDERS FOR TOOTHPICKS, MATCHES OR HAIRPINS

A. This pattern is a primitive design from the South Pacific Islands.

B. Particular care should be taken to cut the grooves of uniform width. The crosses in the background are merely lines stabbed four times with the point of the knife at the intersection of the cross. In making any carving having radiating chips as in this pattern, which is an adaptation of the Greek honeysuckle, care must be taken to make the center of radiation as perfect as possible.

C. Sparklets may be added to the shallow chips to suggest a plant form.

8

7-7/8 x 3 x 3/8

— SHALLOW

— DEEP

— DEEPER

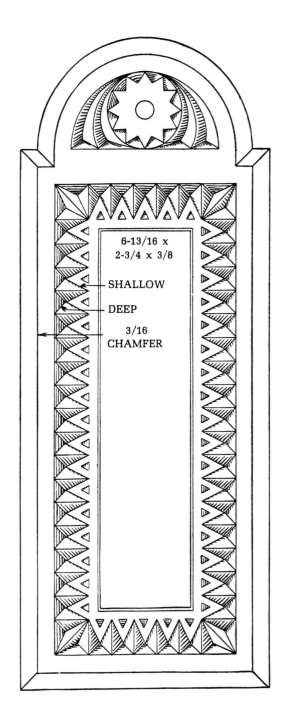

6-13/16 x
2-3/4 x 3/8

— SHALLOW

— DEEP

3/16
CHAMFER

Projects 6 and 7
THERMOMETER MOUNTS

These mounts are designed for thermometers measuring 4″ x 1″. They should, of course, be changed to fit other sizes which may be used. Because of the direction of the grain, care must be taken not to break the slender points of the flat surface in the border design of the shorter mount.

In the longer mount, other methods of cutting chips on this lay-out can be discovered.

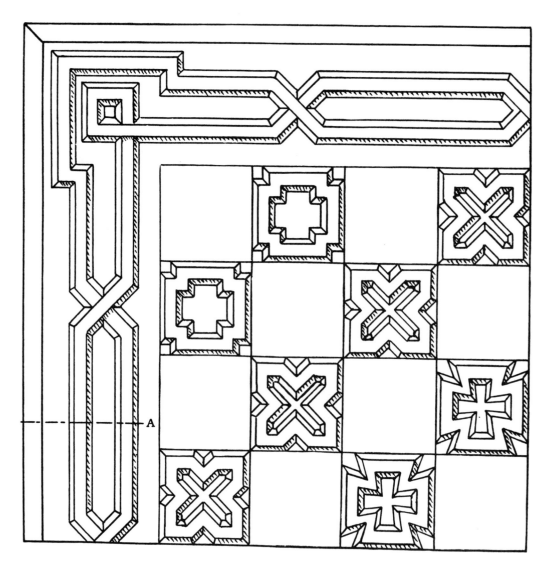

ONE QUARTER OF BOARD

Section A

BOARD 11 x 11 x 7/8

Project 8
CHECKERBOARD

This form of carving, sometimes called ribbon carving, permits the easy sliding of the checkers. The chip slants from the outer line to the next outer line. When selecting material for this checkerboard, avoid any wood that is liable to warp. Well-seasoned mahogany is recommended.

BOTTOM

SIDE

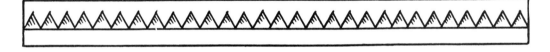

END

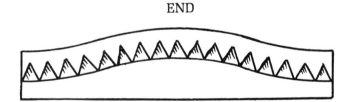

BOTTOM 5-3/4 x 4 x 3/16
SIDE 5-1/2 x 1/2 x 3/16
END 3-3/8 x 3/4 x 3/16

Project 9
PIN TRAY

The diamond rosette should be cut rather shallow. There are many other interesting modes of cutting on such a lay-out. This form was chosen to keep the surface as level as possible.

FRONT (HALF)

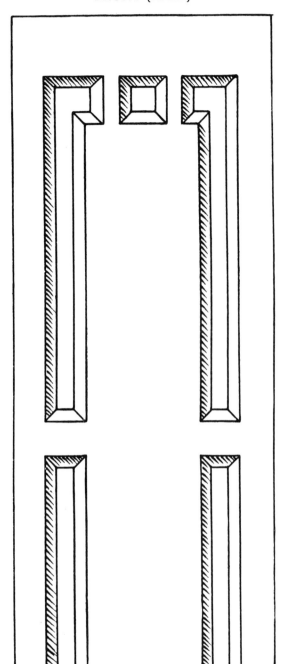

END

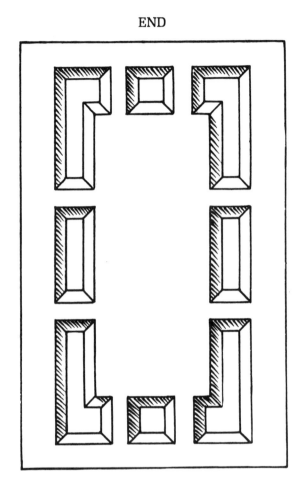

Project 10
GLOVE BOX

The carving on this box represents an interesting variation of grooving. The outer line of the pattern represents a vertical wall about 3/32″ deep, and should be cut first with the knife held vertically. The chip is cut slanting from the next line to this vertical wall. Only one-half of the front and top patterns is shown. The front and end shown in the drawing are the parts below the cover. If a lock is added to this box the front pattern should be modified to accommodate the keyhole. A box like this should be glued and bradded together completely and then the cover sawed apart along the line of separation; 3/16″ is allowed for this.

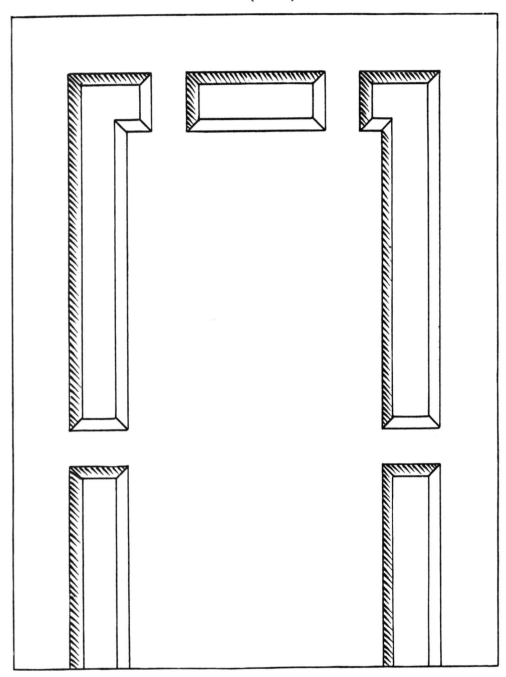

TOP 13-3/4 x 5-1/4 x 3/8

FRONT 13-3/4 x 2-13/16 x 3/4

END 4-1/2 x 2-13/16 x 3/8

3/16 is allowed for sawing apart
the box to form cover.

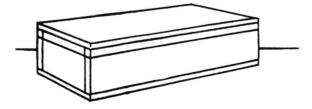

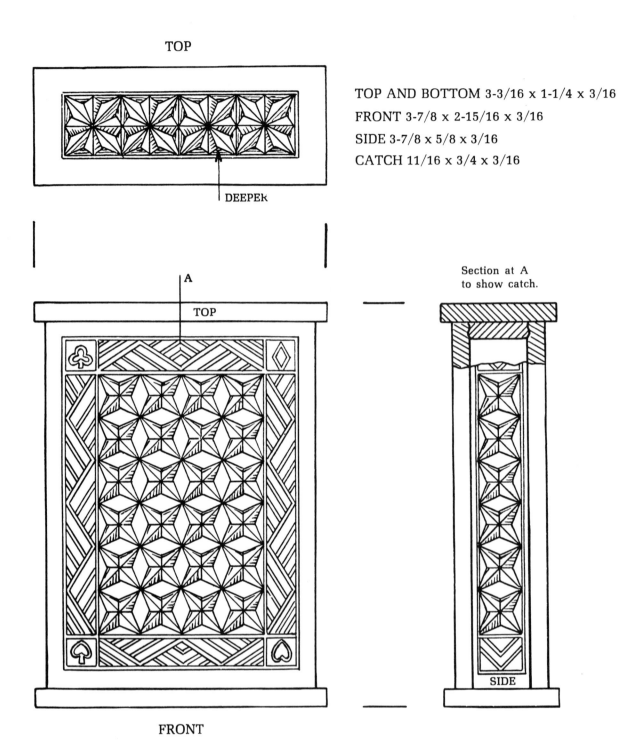

TOP

TOP AND BOTTOM 3-3/16 x 1-1/4 x 3/16

FRONT 3-7/8 x 2-15/16 x 3/16

SIDE 3-7/8 x 5/8 x 3/16

CATCH 11/16 x 3/4 x 3/16

DEEPER

A

TOP

Section at A
to show catch.

SIDE

FRONT

Project 11
CARD CASE

The case should be planned to fit the pack of cards used. The dimensions suggested fit some of the standard sizes. The catch depends upon springing the front and the back apart as the cover is pressed down. If carefully made, it holds the cover well.

TOP 4-1/2 x 3 x 1/4

3-3/4 radius

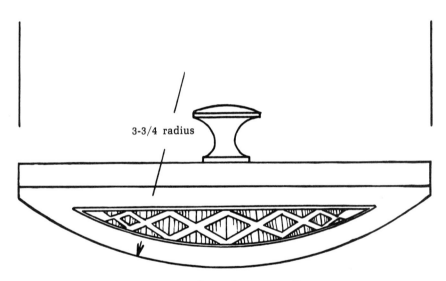

ROCKER 4-1/2 x 3 x 7/8

Project 12
BLOTTER

It is desirable to use a 1/8″ chisel to stab the valley between the rows of diamonds.
A brad awl might be sharpened for this purpose; a knife will stab it in two operations.

HALF OF SHELF

BACK 9 x 7 x 1/2
SHELF 9 x 3 x 1/2
BRACKET 4 x 2 x 1/2

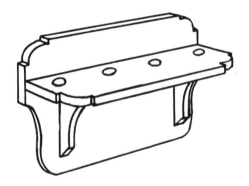

Project 13
PIPE RACK

The holes in the shelf should be of suitable size to accommodate the pipes used. The upper edges of these holes should be well rounded and smooth. The long sweeping valleys in the back can be stabbed by drawing the knife point several times along these lines. To remove the chips smoothly will require several operations. The three small diamond-shaped surfaces at the left and right ends of the back piece are even with the main surface of the board and are simply stabbed on all four sides to receive the valleys.

16

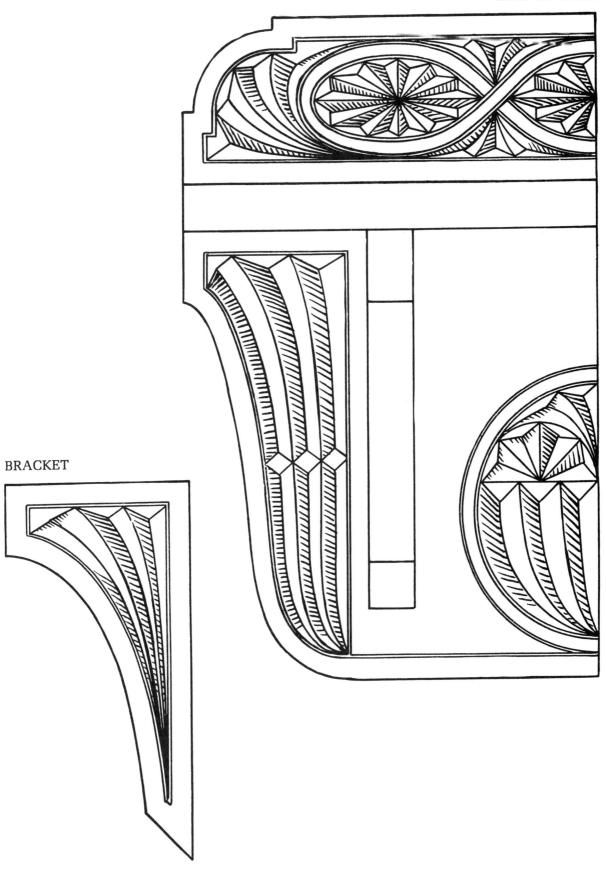

BRACKET

BOARD 10 x 10 x 7/8

Make nine light and nine
dark men of 1/4 dowel 1/4 long

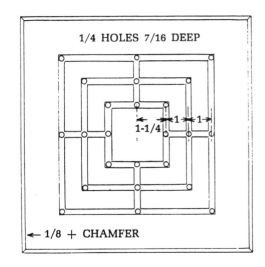

1/4 HOLES 7/16 DEEP

1-1/4

1

1

← 1/8 + CHAMFER

Project 14
PEG MORREL

Peg morrel (nine men's morris, shepherd's mill) is a fine game for two players. (For directions for playing, see p. 2.) The moves are interesting, and victory or defeat may come quickly. The holes in this board are so placed that the game of fox and geese may be made on the reverse side of the board. The pegs should have ends shaped and well sandpapered so that they can readily be inserted into or removed from the holes. A skillful carver would carve the two inner borders on a layout consisting only of the rows of flat (uncut) triangles along their edges. Careful stabbing would finish the design.

BOARD 10 x 10 x 7/8
(may be made on
reverse side of
Peg Morrel board)

Make 15 geese and 1 fox
of 1/4 dowel 1-1/4 long.
Solitaire may be played
with 32 pegs.

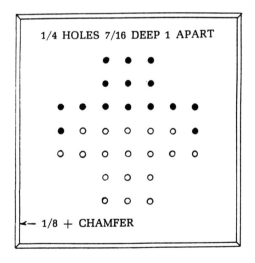

Project 15
FOX AND GEESE

It often adds interest to a piece of decoration if its corresponding members are not exactly the same. This idea is carried out in the long chips along the sides of the board; the valley at the top being straight and the one at the left curved. Sparklets might be introduced in some of the diamonds. (For directions for playing, see p. 2.)

TOP (HALF)

SIDE (HALF)

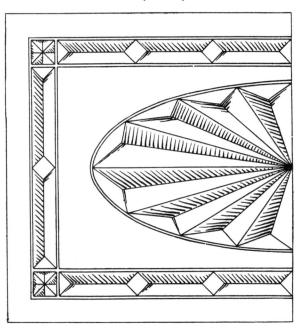

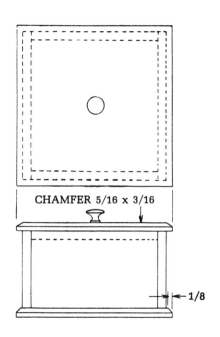

CHAMFER 5/16 x 3/16

1/8

TOP 6-3/4 sq. x 3/8   END 5-1/2 x 3-1/4 x 3/8
SIDE 6-1/4 x 3-1/4 x 3/8   UNDER TOP 5-7/16 sq. x 3/8

Project 16
HANDKERCHIEF BOX

The under top board should be screwed as well as glued to the cover, with the grain running cross-wise. The detail drawings show one-half of one side and one-half of the pattern for the cover.

BACK 6-3/4 x 4-3/4 x 1/4

FRONT 4-3/4 x 4-1/2 x 1/4

SIDE
3-13/16 x 1-1/2 x 1/4

Project 17
WHISKBROOM HOLDER

The front and the back of this model had better be carved before the parts are glued together. Because the design on the sides extends to its edges, the outside rows of chips are better cut after the parts are glued. The chips between the vertical rows of flat diamonds are somewhat peculiar in that their deepest points are not together, but are at opposite ends of the valley.

21

HALF OF FRAME

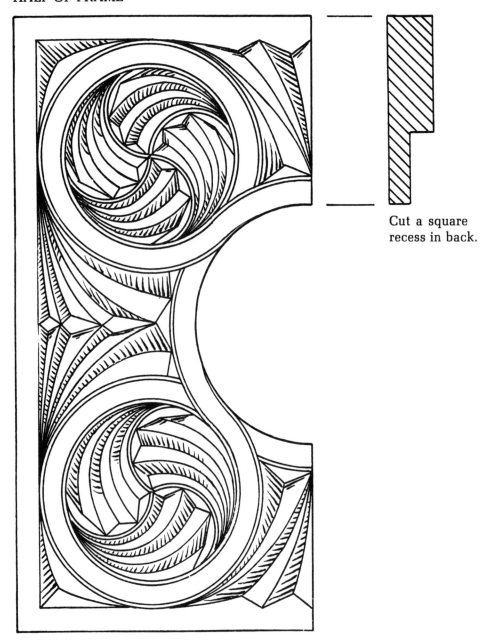

Cut a square
recess in back.

FRAME 6-1/2 x 6-1/2 x 1/2

Project 18
PICTURE FRAME

The recess for the picture should be cut with chisel and router plane before the carving is executed. The circular opening can be cut with a large expansive bit or with a scroll saw. If the frame is to hang on the wall a small brass screw-eye may be used.

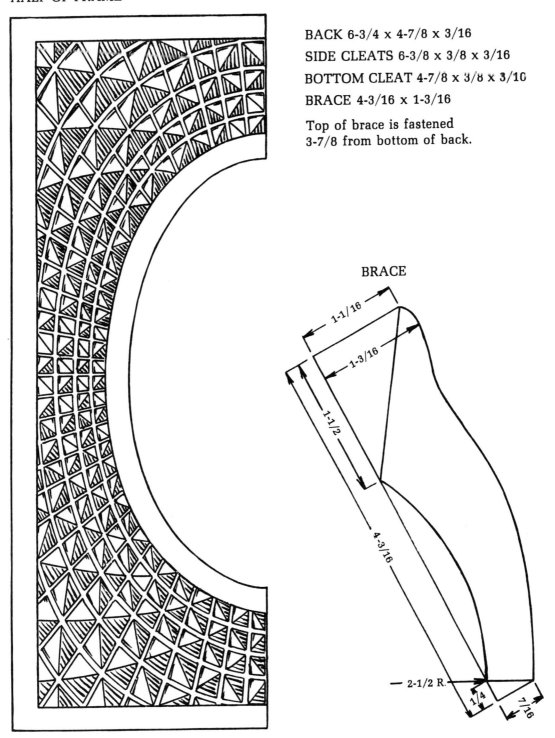

BACK 6-3/4 x 4-7/8 x 3/16

SIDE CLEATS 6-3/8 x 3/8 x 3/16

BOTTOM CLEAT 4-7/8 x 3/8 x 3/16

BRACE 4-3/16 x 1-3/16

Top of brace is fastened
3-7/8 from bottom of back.

BRACE

Project 19
PHOTOGRAPH FRAME

The play of light and shade on this design when carved is much more interesting than the drawing suggests. The carving should be kept delicate, hence the flat radiating and elliptical bands must be made narrow. The narrower they are, however, the more liable to split are those which run across the grain. A pocket into which the photograph slips is built on the back. The brace presupposes the use of the frame as an easel.

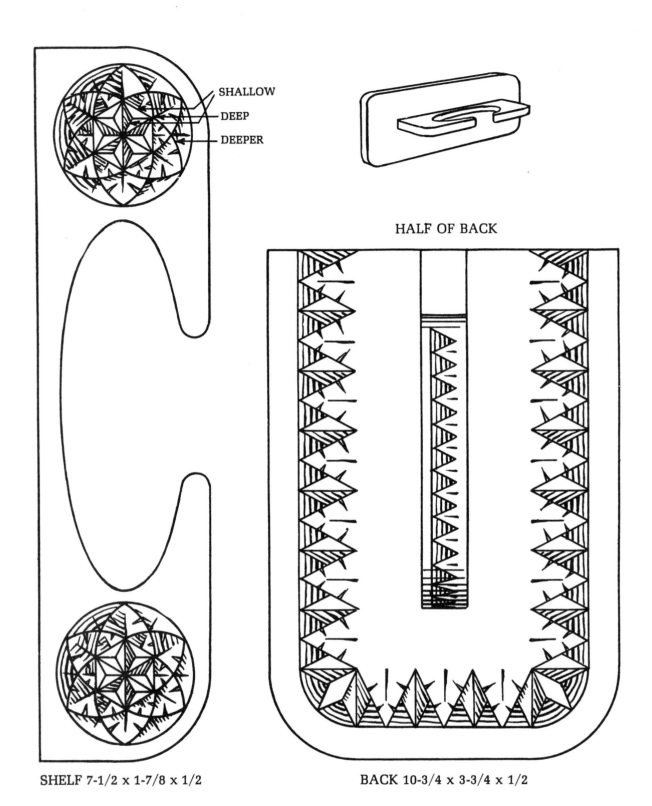

SHALLOW

DEEP

DEEPER

HALF OF BACK

SHELF 7-1/2 x 1-7/8 x 1/2

BACK 10-3/4 x 3-3/4 x 1/2

Project 20
WHISKBROOM HOLDER

To stab these rosettes a gouge (Fig. 6) of suitable sweep is desirable, although the curves can be cut by drawing the knife several times along them. Attention is called to the leaf pattern border on the edge and ends of the shelf. This border may, of course, be omitted. Accurate cutting of the sparklets will add much to the appearance of this article. The upper edges of the elliptical opening should be well rounded with sandpaper.

A 7 x 7/8 x 3/16   B 8 x 1-1/4 x 1/4   C 11 x 1-3/8 x 1/4

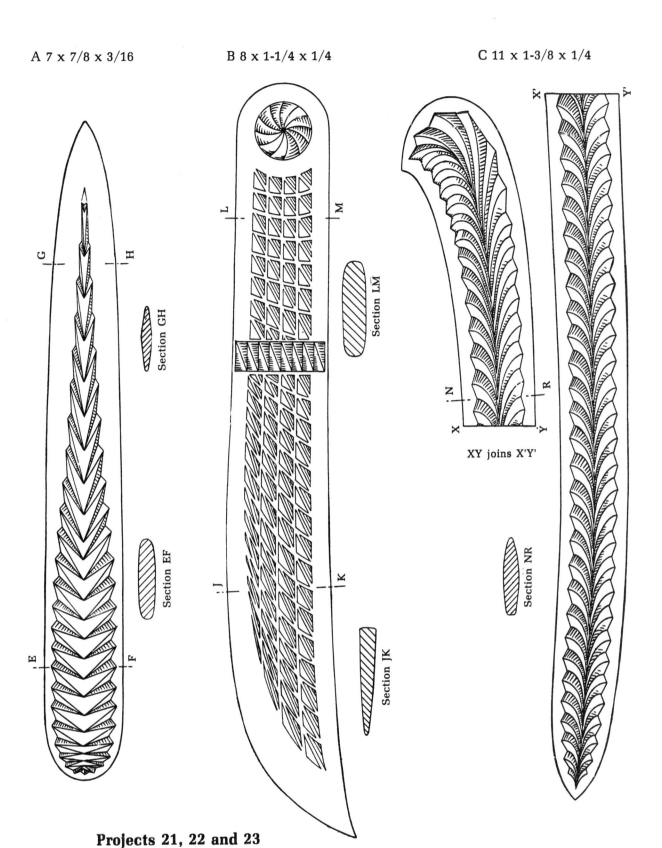

Projects 21, 22 and 23
LETTER OPENERS

These knives should be shaped completely before the carving is added. They should be made of firm, close-grain wood. The design of B was adapted from a paddle from the South Pacific islands; the design of C (to be carved in one piece) from a knife by Jenny Andréen in her book, *Chip-Carving Patterns*.

PLAN OF BOTTOM

WEDGE
(full size)

67-1/2°

3/8

7/16

1-1/2

LACING
WEDGE
SIDE

SIDE

BOTTOM 6 x 6 x 3/4

8 SIDES 12 x 2-3/8 x 3/8

8 WEDGES 1-1/2 x 7/16 x 3/8

SCREW   BOTTOM

Project 24
WASTE BASKET

The octagonal bottom should be made as accurate as possible. The wedges between the eight vertical sides are best made in one long piece. They should be glued and nailed in place before the sides are screwed to the bottom. Only one screw should be put in each side until the tops are tied together. Two rosettes may give place to large brass ring handles. Finally, the sides should be laced together with raw-hide shoe or belt lacings.

SIDE

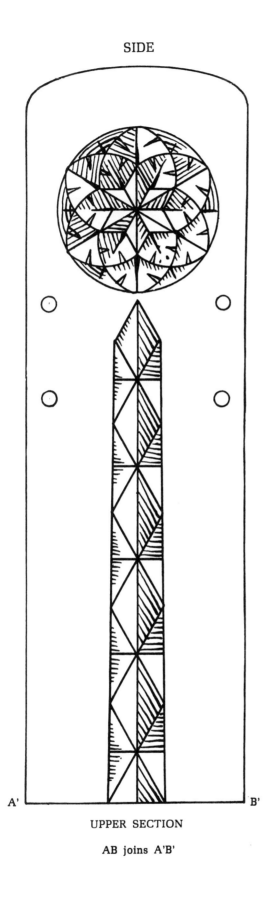

A' B'

UPPER SECTION

AB joins A'B'

AN EASIER ROSETTE

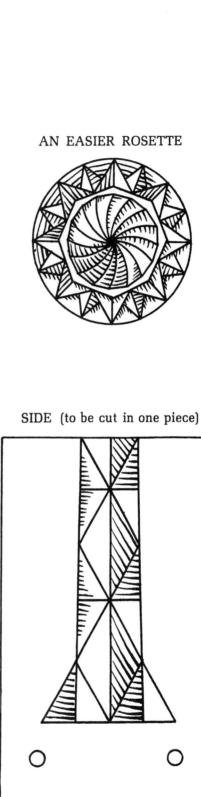

SIDE (to be cut in one piece)

A B

LOWER SECTION

Priscilla sewing cabinet made and carved by Harris W. Moore (black mahogany, oil finish).

DIMENSIONS OF CABINET
2 ENDS 10-3/4 x 8-1/2 x 1/2
*2 SIDES 11 x 5-1/2 x 1/2
2 LIDS 10-15/16 x 3-7/8 x 1/2

*1 TOP 11 x 1-1/2 x 1/2
*1 BOTTOM 11 x 5-9/16 x 1/2
1 HANDLE 12-1/8 x 1-1/2 x 1/2
*Length if bradded; if joined add tenons.

Project 25
PRISCILLA SEWING CABINET

The decoration of this cabinet offers an example of flowing lines embodied in chip carving. If it seems over-elaborate, the author hopes that it will be suggestive to the reader in designing his own pattern. The grids show how any pattern may be fitted into the space to be decorated. The several parts should be carved before they are assembled.

HANDLE (HALF)

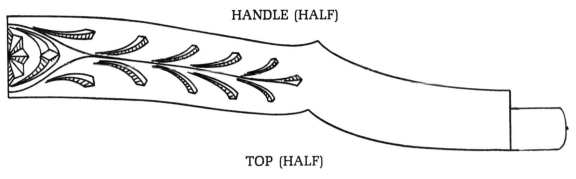

TOP (HALF)

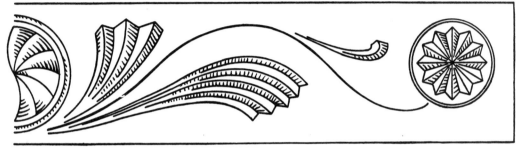

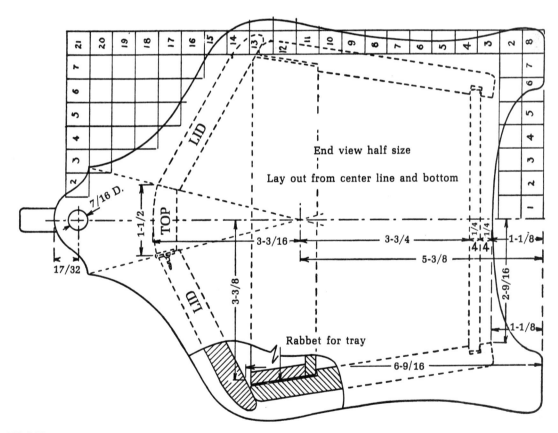

End view half size

Lay out from center line and bottom

7/16 D.

17/32

LID

TOP

LID

1-1/2

3-3/8

3-3/16

3-3/4

5-3/8

1/4 1/4

4 4

1-1/8

2-9/16

1-1/8

Rabbet for tray

6-9/16

TRAY

2 SIDES 10-13/16 x 3/16 x 1/4

2 ENDS 6-3/8 x 1-3/16 x 1/4

1 BOTTOM 10-13/16 x 1-3/16 x 1/4

1 HANDLE 10-5/16 x 1-7/8 x 1/4

2 PARTITIONS 3-1/16 x 1-3/16 x 1/4

TRAY

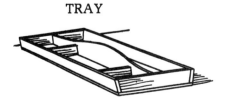

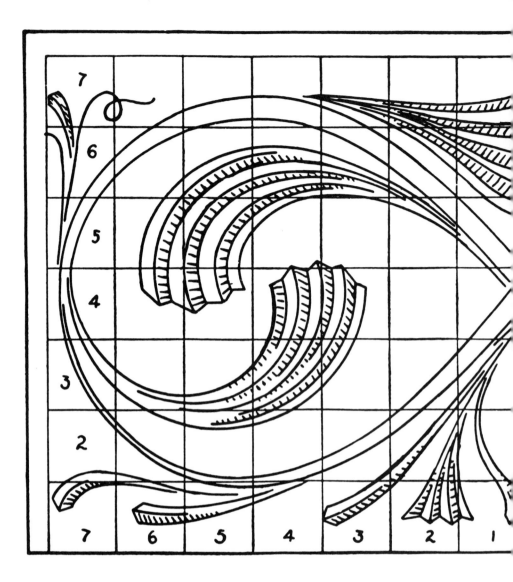

ROSETTE

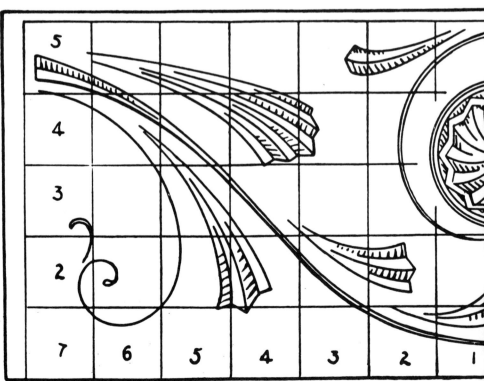

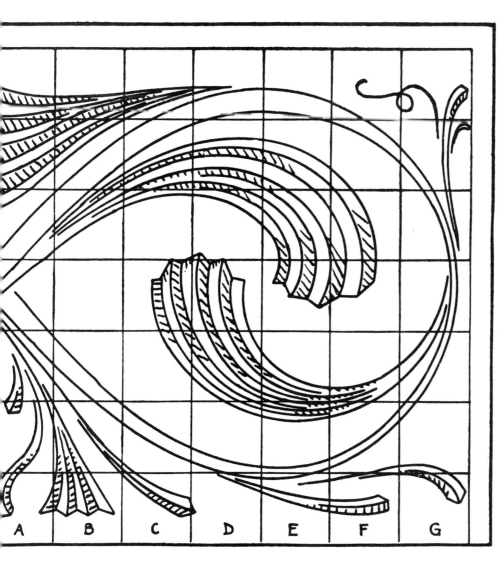

SIDE

A   B   C   D   E   F   G

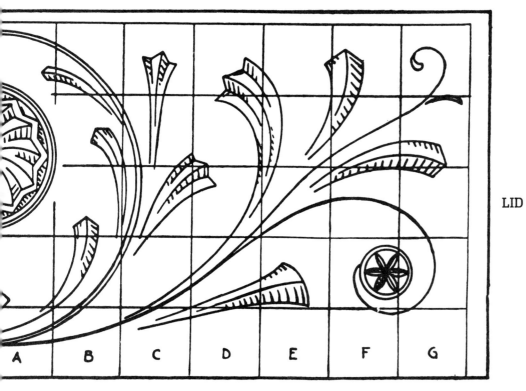

LID

A   B   C   D   E   F   G

END

2-1/2
D.

21
20
19
18
17
16
15
14
13
12
11
10
9
8
7
6
5
4
3
2
1 2 3 4 5 6 7 8 9 10 11 12 13 14 15